P9-AFI-080

THE TIN CAN and Other Poems

William Jay Smith

THE TIN CAN

and Other Poems

A Seymour Lawrence Book

Delacorte Press

Certain of these poems have appeared in the following magazines and anthologies: *Approach; The Berkshire Review; The Carleton Miscellany; Festschrift for Marianne Moore's Seventy-seventh Birthday*, edited by Tambimuttu (Tambimuttu and Mass); *The Hollins Critic; Southern Poetry Today*, edited by Guy Owen and William E. Taylor (Deland, Florida, 1962); *Virginia Quarterly Review; Voices*; and the *Washington Star Sunday Magazine*.

The following poems appeared originally in *The New Republic*: "Funeral" (under the title "Pompes Funèbres"), "The Lovers," "The Antimacassar and the Ottoman," "Petits Chevaux: the Twenties," "Slave Bracelets."

The poems "Morels" and "Random Generation of English Sentences Or, The Revenge of the Poets" appeared originally in *The New Yorker*.

"The Arrow" and "Marcel Proust" appeared originally in *The New York Times*, © 1961, 1962 by The New York Times Company. Reprinted by permission.

The following poems appeared originally in *Poetry*: "Ballad of the Lady Quid Pro Quo," "Northern Lights," "Quail in Autumn," "Riddles," "A Tune for the Teletype," "The Tin Can."

"Where the Rivers Meet" appeared originally in the *Washington University Magazine*, November 1962.

The author and the publishers thank the editors of these publications for permission to reprint.

The translations from the Russian of Andrei Voznesensky are printed with permission of the publishers from *Anti-Worlds: the Poetry of Andrei Voznesensky*, edited by Patricia Blake and Max Hayward (Basic Books). These translations were done in collaboration with Mr. Max Hayward, to whom the author is indebted for many suggestions in phrasing.

FOR *Robert and Helen Allen*

Contents

I · NORTHERN LIGHTS

3 Morels
5 Slave Bracelets
9 Northern Lights
12 Where the Rivers Meet
15 An Observation
17 The Tempest

II · THE WOMAN ON THE PORCH

21 The Lovers
23 The Woman on the Porch
23 The Arrow
24 Marcel Proust
25 Riddles
26 Petits Chevaux: The Twenties
27 Fisher King
28 Dachshunds
29 Quail in Autumn

III · THE ANGRY MAN

33 The Angry Man
36 A Picture of Her Bones
37 The Idiot below the El
38 Funeral

39 Barber, Wartime

40 Five Poems by Andrei Voznesensky

40 NEW YORK AIRPORT AT NIGHT

42 STRIPTEASE

43 WALL OF DEATH

44 ITALIAN GARAGE

45 HER SHOES

IV · A TUNE FOR THE TELETYPE

49 A Friend Laughing

51 A Tune for the Teletype

52 Random Generation of English Sentences
    Or, The Revenge of the Poets

53 Pidgin Pinch

54 The Antimacassar and the Ottoman

56 Bay-Breasted Barge Bird

57 Ballad of the Lady Quid Pro Quo

V · THE TIN CAN

63 The Tin Can

I

Northern
Lights

MORELS

A wet gray day—rain falling slowly, mist over the
    valley, mountains dark circumflex smudges in the distance—

Apple blossoms just gone by, the branches feathery still
    as if fluttering with half-visible antennae—

A day in May like so many in these green mountains, and
    I went out just as I had last year

At the same time, and found them there under the big maples—
    by the bend in the road—right where they had stood

Last year and the year before that, risen from the dark duff
    of the woods, emerging at odd angles

From spores hidden by curled and matted leaves, a fringe of
    rain on the grass around them,

Beads of rain on the mounded leaves and mosses round them,

Not in a ring themselves but ringed by jack-in-the-pulpits
    with deep eggplant-colored stripes;

Not ringed but rare, not gilled but polyp-like, having
    sprung up overnight—

These mushrooms of the gods, resembling human organs
    uprooted, rooted only on the air,

Looking like lungs wrenched from the human body, lungs
    reversed, not breathing internally

But being the externalization of breath itself, these
    spicy, twisted cones,

These perforated brown-white asparagus tips—these morels,
    smelling of wet graham crackers mixed with maple leaves;

And, reaching down by the pale green fern shoots, I nipped
    their pulpy stems at the base

And dropped them into a paper bag—a damp brown bag (their
    color)—and carried

Them (weighing absolutely nothing) down the hill and into
    the house; you held them

Under cold bubbling water and sliced them with a surgeon's
    stroke clean through,

And sautéed them over a low flame, butter-brown; and we ate
    them then and there—

Tasting of the sweet damp woods and of the rain one inch
    above the meadow:

It was like feasting upon air.

SLAVE BRACELETS

I

You wore six bracelets—all of silver—and they moved on your
      wrist as you moved,

Catching the light, drawing it endlessly up and down in coils as
      you walked,

Bringing light in from the far corners of the room, bearing it
      in coils, cutting it in disks as you moved,

Peeling silver from mirrors, slicing the shadows; and when you
      held out your arm and drew it back,

The bracelets, tapping one upon the other, broke through the
      pebbled hours,

Slowly composing a pattern of continuing sound that I could follow
      clearly from room to room;

And the constant click of bracelets filled every crevice with silver.

II

A wash of silver! On that balcony overlooking the Caribbean I sat,
      and the water

Was a field of broken blue-green on which clouds massed and hovered
      in corners like paws,

And one triangular sail flitted and dipped, a checkered moth, over
      a crimson patch;

And the waves broke on a fringe of coral reef below, sweeping up
      over a circle of sand,

And the sound of breakers rose over my head, billowing out from the
      triangular tin roof protruding above the water,

Echoing dizzily through the green light; and below on the sand I
      followed the fine print of a crab darting in and out of his
      hole with every wave,

Tracing with each movement a slender radiating web, erased, then
  recomposed;

And again the combers climbed, and again your bracelets with their
  tapping radiantly caught

In the tail of my eye; the sea became a battery of bangles, a
  heap of polished abalone, uncoiling in profusion,

Splintering in silver at the day's dim edges, beached in delight
  upon the afternoon.

III

A fountain of energy had sprung up beneath my feet, and was playing
  through my veins; the island

Moved with the sea breeze; abandoned windmills on the coral hummocks
  turned in the imagination;

The ebony—that tree called "woman's tongue"—rattled its dry pods;

The banana clattered its gaudy green leaves like so many machetes;
  frangipani uplifted its clumps of coral branches;

Palm trees inclined; pawpaws trembled; wheelbarrows of fern, guided by
  dark hands, came past

And the island was all in motion, but at rest; the sky, drifting off,
  was caught at the edge of a cane field

By a grove of casuarinas, tall and feathery, planted in dark rows to
  catch the rain,

Drawing water from the air to return it to the underlying levels of
  the porous island,

Sweet water seeping down to rest, shimmering-clear, upon the salt,
  filtering out through the cane, emerging in black pools on the
  blond sand

So that all the island rested upon water—layer on layer—feeling
  upon feeling—buoyant and balanced.

IV

With the continuous tapping of your bracelets, I began to compose
    a whole category of sinuous objects,

To detail an inventory of coiling images, of chains whose links
    rose slowly through consciousness,

Rivers meandering in mystical meadows, columns of smoke
    encircling unscaled mountains;

I followed with Australian tribes the parabola of the emu's egg across
    the sky—

Saw how, landing far off in a pile of kindling, it set fire to the
    sun;

I dug deep beside the legendary Papuan and uncovered with him the
    small bright object,

Which, slipping from our hands, climbed into the sky to become the
    moon.

I set out with Dionysus to visit the islands, and abducted with him
    by pirates, was tied with heavy cords

Only to see the knots loosen miraculously and fall to the deck;

Watched the face of the terrified pilot when he sensed that their
    captive was divine,

And the obdurate pirates still refused his release; saw the water
    darken about the ship,

Flowing freely into fragrant wine, while up from the deck, its
    branches enveloping the sail, a vine rose, looping its firm
    trunk around the mast,

And at my side, beneath great pendant clusters, under crisp, veined
    leaves

The god assumed his fearful aspect, and the sailors in horror leapt
    into the sea,

Where, as dolphins, they followed along in the somber water; and
    only the pilot survived.

V

Coils of sound uncoiling, loop on silver loop, circle of light on
       light—

Layer on layer! A crinkling serpent slithered through the shadows,
       nearer and nearer, always eluding me, twisting up through the
       mind's incalculable levels;

And I saw you then, a statuette poised against blue-green water,

A Cretan goddess, whose corsage exposed her small white breasts,
       her lapis lazuli, flounced blue skirts hooped over her waist,

Her arms extending rigidly down before her, serpents of gold and silver
       descending each arm into the resonant shadows,

Each neck held firmly between her fingers, the triangular heads
       thrust upward

—While the triangular tin roof behind you reflected the climbing
       breakers—

Each serpent clasped as if forever, its bright fangs reaching
       resolutely upward, uniting heaven and earth.

NORTHERN LIGHTS

I

I stepped out here on the mountainside, and saw the
     northern lights, cold-clear, clear-white, blue-green, long
     quivering gold knives of light shooting up, cutting the
     sky the horizon round.

Up from the valley mist rose in waves, shot up in steady puffs,
     clear-cold in the light,

And in places all the sky seemed made of moving skeins of white
     hair rising water-clear, stars tangled in the flowing strands.

The brook ran below (it was August, but cold); and I could hear
     its chill, pebbled water bubbling down, close in upon my ear.

Crickety night sounds: black trees came spangled forth, while
     behind a moving green gold turned them into shaggy hulks
     heaving in waves of light.

Trees stood, but moved, bearded and blowing, but no wind blew,
     and the dark itself moved, kept moving with light.

II

Mist, held deep in the valley in layers chalk-white, sheet-white,
     hung billowing between rock walls;

And still it rose, shade becoming light, light, shade, and as I
     stepped into the field, grass also moved, brightened by all
     these waves of hairy light.

The mountain pool caught, and tried to hold, patches of moving
     light, and the water, coming down from the mountain, rang,
     swinging clear

Over evergreens overgrown; ribbons of willow, beside or behind
     or above the pool, leaned, moved, kept clear-turning until
     the whole sky moved; and I stepped into an ever-deepening
     river of grass, green-moving and slow, glowworm-light
     expanding and wavering.

Thin blades of green cut through blue-green, or green upon white,
  white upon gray, green upon mist-yellow, green and primrose-
  yellow.

And primroses beside the rockpool, chill yellow in the moving
  mist; and light kept coming by while I moved with light
  moving, stood (leapt), reached (held) earth-air (whole-part),
  clear-cold and all-white.

III

I stepped forth, calm but much shaken: no night there ever had
  been so mist-torn, mountain-white.

The Milky Way had broken loose, and spun, a real web, round and
  round until the milk strands tore loose, and hung dangling
  above the valley.

A black dog lay by the road's edge, by a branch from a tree
  fallen, unmoving, shaggy with mist;

The dark barn jutted forth, its peak a prow, against the buffalo-
  humped mountains, and

In all innocence this night broke clear, sailing, sails trimmed
  and taut, no longer beclouded and cloud-tossed, but coming
  through, all clear.

IV

An August night: Jupiter off there in blowing, blissful mist-light.

It was cold; and sheer puffs, seemingly unpropelled, kept
  coming up and out until the whole sky was moving, nacreous
  and white—

All over mother-of-pearl, but pearl yet unformed, not white, but
  blue-rippling pearl-shell, caught up and streaming, moss-green,
  salmon-pink, and shaken.

Drunken, shivering, cold-quaking, I stood, moving skyward, still
  drinking deep draughts shimmering and milk-white.

V

The sky was a moving bowl, hairy and white, with the stars chiselled
and chipped, spinning in the whole sky.

And the sky was rinsed clear, while the brook rushed on below,
cleaving night sounds.

And the whole night moved, an upturned bowl, as if the soul itself
had been washed clear

Of all entanglements, and shone forth, fresh-clean, overturned and
opalescent.

It was as if the soul alone could speak, and having spoken, rippled,
rubbed, and crossed, had been drained of speech

And shone forth new-clean, clear-cold, and white, with nothing now
within to hold or hide . . .

And I brushed the blowing skeins of light from my face, stepped
back and shut the door, and went inside.

WHERE THE RIVERS MEET

*On the Inauguration of Thomas Hopkinson Eliot as
    Chancellor of Washington University
        12 October 1962*

Here where the winding rivers meet,
What is it that the autumn air,
So full and fine, so bittersweet,
      Would clearly now declare?
Queen Anne's lace and goldenrod
That grace this bright Columbus day—
Unto what Glory do they nod?
      What have they now to say?
The regal pheasant, dove, and quail,
The cardinals and flashing jays,
Met with on an Ozark trail—
      What is it now they praise?

Those rivers that no dark can dim—
The Meramec, the Gasconade—
Where summer-long I used to swim,
      And other boys now wade;
That gravel bank, that clear, cold spring,
Where, shaded, pensively I sat
And fished for crawfish on a string
      With strips of bacon fat;
Those lean-tos built of sassafras,
Tents pitched with wobbly sumac poles,
Those caverns reached through fern and grass
      By frightening sinkholes,—

Remembered places that I see,
Persimmons ripened on a bough,
But riper now in memory—
      What have they to avow?
St. Louis, birthplace of the blues,
Of T. S. Eliot, Eugene Field,

Producer of good beer and shoes,
        Of Prophets unrevealed,
St. Louis, you whose every haunt
I used to know—your parks, your drives,
The shanties on your riverfront,
        Your mansions and your dives,—

City, whose spirit once possessed
Charles Lindbergh the moment he
Brought his rickety plane to rest,—
        What would you have us see?
City, whose every thoroughfare—
Broadway and Olive, Delmar, Grand—
Leads to that central fountain, where,
        A flower in his hand,
Mississippi strides to meet
Missouri, nude in open court,
While wind-blown fans of spray compete,
        And water-folk cavort,—

Streets that are named for Lafayette,
Pierre Laclede, Auguste Chouteau,
What would you have us not forget,
        What would you let us know?
Streets that I travelled early, late,
And now but faintly recognize,
What is it that they celebrate,
        What do they emphasize?
Remembered streets and fields and flowers,
The rich, rewarding out-of-doors,—
All announce this day is ours,
        This day, our Chancellor's.

And those who have assembled here
To wish him health, long life, and fame,
The red and green of autumn wear,
        To glorify his name;
So may this day of fine converse
In festive hood and somber robe
Be the pivot of their universe,

The center of their globe;
May winter snow and autumn rain
Be all clear weather on their chart;
Reward them with a fertile brain
     And understanding heart.

May they probe wisdom's deepest worth,
The flood of learning never stem,
That they may honor him henceforth
     Who this day honors them.
May every mind and heart explore
The space expanding with the stars
That illuminate this muddy shore,
     These willow-banked sandbars;
And may they brighten all his days
Until each eye enlightened greet
The Chancellor, whom now we praise
     Here where the rivers meet.

AN OBSERVATION

For Marianne Moore on her seventy-seventh birthday

Now every day here at the height of summer
    from the edge of the apple tree bent by
    the weight of its fruit so that the whole thing

Is criss-crossed with strings of small green apples,
    looped every which way up and down and in and
    out—

Through the midday haze against the mountains swathed
    now in a gray-blue gauze of heat—

From the heart of the apple tree, its bark mottled and
    warped, its branches hooked and looking half-
    hollow—

From the hunched and dwarfed apple tree, and then from
    deep within the gray-green of the swamp willow—
    as if on a scale up and down its trailing
    branches—

Then high there on the bough of the fat bulging ash, its
    gold keys hanging dry and desperate like the fringe
    of old upholstery—

Now every day when all the other birds and even the
    insects have ceased I hear his chip-chip sweet-sweet
    chew-chew, followed by what sounds like a high *wit*—

Wit—which, as you know, somehow cuts through the heart
    of haze; and see him—a blue gem

Resting within the gray cushions of heat—his blue turning
    in the half-hooded light from indigo to ultramarine
    to azure,

Drawing into his faceted feathered body the gold and olive
    green of the mountains, absorbing as in watercolor all
    the lost color of the heavens

While below him dragonflies beside the elderberry bush dart
their wild blue brooches over the wet velvet surface of
the pond;

See him as you would see him, this New England visitor from
the coast of Cuba, this indigo bunting as more than a
mere jewel—

As a flame breathing at the core of consciousness, fed by
conscience, a poem poised against the shifting dull
gray seasons, asking, in its permanence and rare
felicity, "What are years?"

THE TEMPEST

Let England knowe our willingnesse, for that our worke is goode,
Wee hope to plant a Nation, where none before hath stood.
>   —R. RICH in *Newes from Virginia*

Imagine that July morning: Cape Henry and Virginia
There but one week off; black winds having gathered
All the night before,
The gray clouds thickened, and the storm,
From out the wild Northeast, bore
Down upon them, beating light from heaven.
The cries of all on board were drowned in wind,
And wind in thunder drowned;
With useless sails upwound,
The Sea Adventure rode upon rivers of rain
To no known destination.
Bison-black, white-tongued, the waves
Swept round;
Green-meadow beautiful, the sea below swung up
To meet them, hollow filling hollow,
Till sound absorbed all sound;
Lashed about gnatlike in the dark,
The men with candle flame
Sought out the leaks along the hull.

While oakum spewed, one leak they found
Within the gunnery room, and this they stopped
With slabs of beef;
Their food they fed that leak, that wound,
But it continued still to bleed, and bled
Until its blood was everywhere,
And they could see their own blood
Rush to join it,
And the decks were wet and red;
And greater leaks sprang open in the hold.

Then, on the fourth day, having given up
All but themselves the ship contained—
Trunks, chests, food, firearms, beer and wine—

When they prepared to hack
The mainmast, to batten down all hatches
And commit the vessel to the sea,
They saw far off—sweet introduction of good hope—
A wavering light-green, brooding calm,
Trees moving with the waves—and it was land.

And so the ship rode on, rode out the gale,
And brought them, wrecked but living, to the island there,
Where safely, under more compliant skies,
They might chart out that voyage to a shore
On which with confidence a nation would arise.

II

The Woman on the Porch

THE LOVERS

Above, through lunar woods a goddess flees
Between the curving trunks of slender trees;
Bare Mazda bulbs outline the bone-white rooms

Where, on one elbow, rousing by degrees,
They stare, a sheet loose-folded round their knees,
Off into space, as from Etruscan tombs.

THE WOMAN ON THE PORCH

A woman in my dream sits on a cool front porch,
And there, through the declining afternoon,
Weaves within her mind the threads of my story,
Calling the characters in from the shadows.

Then, weary of conjuring,
As if this light, half-light,
Were in itself too great
To bear, and she were drawn onstage
Before the most receptive of audiences,
She leaves behind my half-completed story,
And walks across the green
Front lawn to the flowerbeds.

Bending above them,
Her eye catching the sun's last flames,
She says: "Flowers are children; when
I see them I want to know their names . . ."

And the flowers answer
And identify themselves—
Rose, carnation, sunflower, camellia,

While night comes down within my dream upon the world,
And the sky, for a brief moment, is the color of currant and quince.

THE ARROW

If body is a bow, and soul the string,
How certain is the arrow of the eye!
Like Zeno's arrow, held within the tumbling
Wing of time, it flies yet cannot fly
Unless through all eternity it fly
And bring down death, an unrelenting lie,
And being conquered, conquer—and so sing!

MARCEL PROUST

His childhood he gave to a public which had none,
And then withdrawing to a cork-lined room,
Lived ever after . . . On his pages sprawl
Sentences like vine leaves on the wall
Of some well-weathered ruin where the sun
Picks out the childlike letters on a tomb.

RIDDLES

1

Within a frame in narrow tinkling strands,
Down-rippling on the body, through the hands,
It hangs as if dividing life from death:
Approach it now, and part it with your breath.

2

In glass contained, and gnawed as if by doubt,
Its tongue uncoiled to drive the shadows out,
How serpent-like upon the crackling air
It broods upon a page of Baudelaire!

3

It dogs your footsteps through the sunny day
Till night comes down and spirits it away;
Lengthening with light, it takes you whole,
Becomes your body and assumes your soul.

4

Earth it rounds with heaven's bloom—
A round of earth in a sunlit room.

5

It leads you a chase through a tangle of words
And gives but the bones when you look for the birds.

ANSWERS TO THE RIDDLES: 1. *Bead Curtain*; 2. *Oil Lamp*; 3. *Shadow*;
4. *Flowerpot*; 5. *Riddle*

PETITS CHEVAUX: THE TWENTIES

I

Harry Crosby one day launched the Bedroom Stakes—
Frivolity out in front, Fidelity overtaken by Concubine.
The play was fast, the bets were high. Who lost? Who won?
Green baize drank the tilting shadows of the sun,
And Death left the players' goblets brimming with blood-red wine.

II

Scott Fitzgerald organized the Crack-up Stakes—
The horses galloped ahead; victrola records turned.
He downed his drink and wrote; wife Zelda whirled and swayed;
The goblets shattered, but the words survived Time's raid,
And Zelda danced on madly till the asylum burned.

FISHER KING

The tall Fijian spears a giant turtle
And hurls him down upon the foaming breakers;
Then rides him over gardens green and fertile
Past huge marine toadstools and pepper-shakers.

What elegance in that superb design,
What native mastery of nerve and eye!
Along the shore, a plumed and nodding line
Of fine-ribbed, slender palm trees flanks the sky.

The waiting island there, an open leaf,
Hangs trembling on the waves, the heavens crack;
While breakers climb the bone-white coral reef,
Triumphantly he rides the ocean back.

So seeing him, I see again at dawn,
Beyond the shifting boundaries of night,
His image, from the dark unconscious drawn,
Come shimmering and powerful to light.

DACHSHUNDS

The Dachshund leads a quiet life
    Not far above the ground;
He takes an elongated wife,
    They travel all around.

They leave the lighted metropole;
    Nor turn to look behind
Upon the headlands of the soul,
    The tundras of the mind.

They climb together through the dusk
    To ask the Lost-and-Found
For information on the stars
    Not far above the ground.

The Dachshunds seem to journey on:
    And following them, I
Take up my monocle, the Moon,
    And gaze into the sky.

Pursuing them with comic art
    Beyond a cosmic goal,
I see the whole within the part,
    The part within the whole;

See planets wheeling overhead,
    Mysterious and slow,
While Morning buckles on his red,
    And on the Dachshunds go.

QUAIL IN AUTUMN

Autumn has turned the dark trees toward the hill;
The wind has ceased; the air is white and chill.
Red leaves no longer dance against your foot,
The branch reverts to tree, the tree to root.

And now in this bare place your step will find
A twig that snaps flintlike against the mind;
Then thundering above your giddy head,
Small quail dart up, through shafting sunlight fled.

Like brightness buried by one's sullen mood
The quail rise startled from the threadbare wood;
A voice, a step, a swift sun-thrust of feather
And earth and air come properly together.

III

The Angry Man

THE ANGRY MAN

El sueño de la razón produce monstruos.
—GOYA

I

Reason slumbers; and in the terrible isolation of my anger I observe
    a thousand monsters of the mind's making;

I wander on a moonscape exploring its tunnels, picking up bits and
    pieces of the past

To hurl at growling beasts that sulk away half-seen; I gaze from a
    steel cage out at a wall rimmed with dragons' teeth,
    observation towers and aprons of barbed wire

Lacing the horizon; eyes peer through the night as through the
    isinglass of old coal stoves;

I am a passenger on a ship in the shape of a carving block
    bearing a cargo of bones;

I know the language spoken by cats and dogs, all peripheral tongues;
    I invent new words, every syllable detailing disaster;

I am the King of Buttons, enriched by bottle-caps, profligate with
    paper;

My voice goes out like a funicular over an abyss, and my hands
    hang at my side, clenching the void;

My dreams are filled with bitter oranges and carrots, signifying
    calumny and sorrow;

And when I awake the windows are outlined in creosote; a network of
    pipes is thrown up around my room and water pours from a
    yellow geyser in the plaster.

II

Reason slumbers; and I go where the world takes me—back upon
    myself; and if I have slept, I awake, projected on a raft
    into a soft green landscape

Where blanched concrete highways keep circling the hillsides in
      whalebone, drinking up the cars through the baleen formed by
      spiny trees against the sunset—

And I am the passenger hurled from the passing car, the driver
      swallowed by the black whale of the world;

And the journey ends where it began: the black whale's mouth opens
      around me into a pleated camera in which my eye is the lens—

And what I see is a world opening into other black mouths—
      gullet to gullet—lens to lens—

And what is recording is recorded, what is seeing, seen; and
      the giant shutter opens always on horror.

III

The monsters of the mind's making have begun their destruction
      and will carry it through;

They keep attacking, throwing iron hoops that encircle my
      ankles, thighs, chest

Until I am bound with iron rope and hung from a precipice; and the
      cliff is no cliff but a ceiling from which hairy roots
      dangle at my side—

Not roots but the branches of trees growing into the air by their
      roots—

Around them dream flowers twisting out—black roses, blue sun-
      flowers following a black sun—

Morning glories, dirt-colored blooms encircling mansarded
      basements—

Skylights opening out like trapdoors into gray cloud caverns in
      which birds dive downward like fish, and television aerials float,
      the skeletons of dangling kites—

Rivers are nailed above me, their bird-fish flying, teeth dragging
      the marbled water, and their debris lining a painted dome of
      tin cans, bottles, rusted and twisting knives;

A bloated piano like a black armadillo bores its way over the
      edges into a cloud

And cemeteries drift overhead like upturned trays held by frozen
    waiters.

IV

The black iron hoops snap and uncoil, coiling me upward, upright,
    backward in time and space;

I am alone in a courtyard in the middle of a desert, holding in my
    hands the coils that have become a whip.

It is dusk, and the air is alive with soft flying creatures;
    I snap the whip at them, looping their bodies, bringing
    them down until the stones of the courtyard are red

And at last the air is quiet and no chirp or whimper is heard
    from any chink or crevice.

I climb the spiral stone steps to a room overlooking the desert;
    and I lie now on an iron cot watching the moon-white sand
    billow out in waves like the sea;

And the whip, having answered unreasoning reason, rests limp
    at my side—a tassel, a tail, a reed.

A PICTURE OF HER BONES

I saw her pelvic bones one April day
After her fall—
Without their leap, without their surge or sway—
I saw her pelvic bones in cold X ray
After her fall.
She lay in bed; the night before she'd lain
On a mat of leaves, black boulders shining
Between the trees, trees that in rain pitched every which way
Below the crumbling wall,
Making shadows where no shadows were,
Writing black on white, white on black,
As in X ray,
While rain came slowly down, and gray
Mist rolled up from the valley.
How still, how far away
That scene is now: the car door
Swinging open above her in the night,
A black tongue hanging over
That abyss, saying nothing into the night,
Saying only that white is black and black is white,
Saying only that there was nothing to say.
No blood, no sound,
No sign of hurt nor harm, nothing in disarray,
Slow rain like tears (the tears have dried away).
I held her bare bones in my hands
While swathed in hospital white she lay;
And hold them still, and still they move
As, tall and proud, she strides today,
The sweet grass brushing her thighs,
A whole wet orchard mirrored in her eyes;—
Or move against me here—
With all their lilt, their spring and surge and sway—
As once they did that other April day
Before her fall.

THE IDIOT BELOW THE EL

From summer's tree the leopard leaves are torn
Like faces from the windows of the train,
And at my foot a mad boy's tweed cap falls,
And no moth's born that can disturb his brain.

The traffic, with a sound of cap and bells,
Winds into his ear; his blunted eyes
Are button-hooks, his tight lips twisted shells,
His fingers, candy canes to snare the flies.

Below, the leaves lie still in wind and rain,
And overhead the rails run on and meet
Somewhere outside of time: the clamor dies;
An iron hoop goes clanking down the street.

FUNERAL

Now he is gone where worms can feed
Upon him, a discarded rind,
God's image, and a thinking reed,
     In blindness blind

As any taxidermist's owl.
He who was tall and fleet and fair
Is now no more; the winds howl,
     The stones stare.

Your double who went dressed in black
And beat the lions to their cage
Lies in blood; the whips crack,
     The beasts rage.

Don your somber herringbone
And clap your top hat to your head.
The carriage waits; the axles groan;
     While prayers are said,

Rest your hot forehead on the plush;
And hear, beyond the measured, sad
Funereal drums, above the hush,
     The lions pad

Intently through some sunless glade,
The body's blood-fed beasts in all
Their fury, while the lifted spade
     Lets earth fall.

BARBER, WARTIME

Seaman First Class, name of Cartocelli,
Clipper-quick, adept at dialects,
Trigger-finger poised above the belly,
Trims the dormant intellects.

Off there, the long white razor of the reef
Slashes lather through the slender trees;
A mynah bird berates a breadfruit leaf,
Light trails, hairy round one's knees.

Off there, in faded blue the men go walking,
There, grim and gray, a dusty lorry comes;
Evening; bugles; and the blur of talking;
And the darker sound of drums.

What are life and death to Cartocelli,
Who shears the domes his dimming glass reflects?
Night falls; men die—to him details are silly,
And trim, the dormant intellects.

FIVE POEMS BY ANDREI VOZNESENSKY

I

New York Airport at Night

FAÇADE

Guardian of heavenly gates, self-portrait, neon retort,
Airport!

Your duralumined plate glass darkly shines
Like an X ray of the soul.

How terrifying
        when the sky in you
        is shot right through with the smouldering tracer-lines
        of far-off capitals!

Round the clock
        your sluice gates
        admit the starred fates
        of porters and prostitutes.

        Like angels in the bar your alcoholics dim;
        Thou speakest with tongues to them.

Thou raisest them up
        who are downcast;
Thou who announcest to them at last:
                "Arrival!"

LANDING AREA

Cavaliers, destinies, suitcases, miracles are awaited . . .
Five Caravelles
        are slated
        dazzlingly to land from the sky.

Five fly-by-night girls wearily lower their landing gear;
Where is the sixth?

She must have gone too far—
             the bitch, the little stork, the star.

Cities dance under her
                    like electric grills.

Where does she hover now,
                    circling around, moaning as though ill,
                    her cigarette glowing in the fog?

It's the weather she doesn't understand;
The ground won't let her land.

THE INTERIOR

The forecast is bad. When a storm looms,
You retreat, as with partisans, into your waiting rooms.

Our rulers snooze
                    in carefree embrace
While the traffic controller, calm as a pharmacist, reroutes them
                                        through the air.

One great eye peers into other worlds,
While with window cleaners
                    like midges your other eyes water.

Crystal giant, parachuted from the stars,
It is sweet but sad
                    to be the scion of a future that sports
Neither idiots
                    nor wedding-cake railway stations—
Only poets and airports!

Groaning within its glass aquarium
The sky
            fits the earth like a drum.

STRUCTURES

Airport—accredited embassy
Of ozone and sun!

A hundred generations
                    have not dared what you have won—
The discarding of supports.

In place of great stone idols
A glass of cool blue
                    without the glass,
Beside the baroque fortresses of savings banks
As antimaterial
                    as gas.

Brooklyn Bridge, rearing its idiot stone, cannot consort
With this monument of the era,
The airport.

II

Striptease

Playing her crazy part,
                    the dancer begins to take all
Her clothes off . . . Do I bawl
Or is it the lights that make my eyes smart?

She rips off a scarf, a shawl, her tinsel and fringe,
As one would slowly peel an orange.

Her eyes like a bird's are haunted with miseries
As she does her "striptease."

It's terrifying. In the bar, wolf-calls, bald pates.
Like leeches with blood
The drunkards' eyes inflate.

That redhead, like someone bespattered with egg yolk,
Is transformed into a pneumatic drill!
The other, a bedbug,
                    is horrible and apoplectic;
And the saxophone howls on, apocalyptic.

Universe, I curse your lack of edges,
And the Martian lights on your sweeping bridges;
I curse you,
                    adoring and marvelling, as
This downpour of woman responds to jazz.

"Are you America?" I'll ask like an idiot;
She'll sit down, tap her cigarette.

"Are you kidding, kiddo?" she'll answer me.
"Better make mine a double martini!"

III

Wall of Death

Casting her spell and daring death,
A woman zooms round the wall of death!
With leather leggings
                 as red as crab's claws,
And wicked red lips that give one pause,
She hurtles—horizontal torpedo—
A chrysanthemum stuck in her belt.

Atomic angel, Amazon,
With cratered cheeks indrawn,
Your motorcycle passes overhead,
Its noise, a power saw's.

Living vertically is such a bore,
Darling barbarian, daughter of Icarus . . .
It's the plight
Only of vestal virgin and suburbanite
To live vertical and upright.

In this creature who soars
Over awnings, ovations, posters, and jeers
I now can see
                 the horizontal essence of woman
Float before me!

Ah, how her orbit whirls her round the wall,
Her tears nailed to each eyeball;
And her trainer, Singichants,
Bullies her like Genghis Khan . . .

Says Singichants: "Let me tell you I
Have my hands full with that one, plastered up there like a fly!

And yesterday she had a flat . . . the little schemer . . . 'I'll write
                              to the boss,' says she;
And claws at my face like a mad gypsy."

During intermission I make my way
To her . . . "Instruct me in the horizontal!" I say.

But she stands there like lead,
The Amazon, and shakes her head;
Still shaking, dizzy from the wall,
Her eyes blurred with
                    such longing
                              for the horizontal!

IV

Italian Garage

To Bela Akhmadulina

The floor's a mosaic—
A trout's back stippled with light.

The garage in the palazzo sleeps.
                              It is night.

In rows the motorcycles rest
Like Saracens or slumbering locusts.

No Paolos here, no Juliets—
Only Chevrolets that pant and sweat.

Figures in the Giotto frescoes are
Like mechanics mirrored in each car.

Ghosts of feuds and battles range at large;
What do you summon in your dreams, garage?

Is it halberds
              or tyrants that haunt
You? Or women
                  picked up in restaurants?

One motorcycle seems to brood—
The reddest of the little brood.

Why is it still awake? Is it because
Tomorrow is Christmas and tomorrow it will crash?

Oranges, applause . . .
                                        Those who smash
Themselves to pieces never die.

Give her the gun, doomed one, blood-red!
And for the girl who rides you it's too bad.

We were not born to survive, alas,
But to step on the gas.

V

Her Shoes

(from OZA)

When I walk in the park or swim in the sea,
A pair of her shoes waits there on the floor.

The left one leaning on the right,
Not enough time to set them straight.

The world is pitch-black, cold and desolate,
But they are still warm, right off her feet.

The soles of her feet left the insides dark,
The gold of the trademark has rubbed off.

A pair of red doves pecking seed,
They make me dizzy, rob me of sleep.

I see the shoes when I go to the beach
Like those of a bather drowned in the sea.

Where are you, bather? The beaches are clean.
Where are you dancing? With whom do you swim?

In a world of metal, on a planet of black,
Those silly shoes look to me like

Doves perched in the path of a tank, frail
And dainty, as delicate as eggshell.

IV

A Tune for the Teletype

A FRIEND LAUGHING

For N. B.

I

What wardroom could hold your laughter? What ship sustain the
broadsides of your mirth?

Captain of comedy, clasping and unclasping your hands, face
immobile, brown moustache twinkling, eyes brighter than
wind-driven water,

Commanding life and us your captives, you lead us on over poorly
caulked and pitching decks, waves mounting on every side,

Shoulders hunched, striding slowly forward, hands erratic sprung
compasses, outlining our impossible course,

Your voice building story within story—fleet after fleet
destroyed, great masts crumbling, hulls aflame, sails ablaze,
the swollen sun, a bubble of blood—

Tale after tale opening out into the sky, one cloud card-castle
after another, until they all collapse and our bright faces,
following you, are set adrift, and there is no rescue but
laughter.

Navigator, sailor, fisherman, whose greatest catch is in the nets
of foolery,

Titan of timing, sultan of slapstick, knowing that laughter always
creates its own occasion

And that the clown can smell the person he's talking to even over
the telephone,

Tentative and shy, knowing that laughter hurts as well as heals,
protector of one-eared rabbits and of dogs shaggy and silly,

Bringer of brightness, all Indian tribes are released from their
reservations when you utter their names,

All drugstore Indians are lined up and set in motion in a comic
carrousel;

The badlands of boredom are invaded by your posses of parody, and
the dunces left dithering on the dunes when you are by words
possessed!

Painter, whose every deadpan expression like the "Nude Descending"
becomes "an explosion in a shingle factory,"

Elegant, dignified, but in laughter always undignified, knowing
that only in smiling there is dignity, not in laughter,

Clutching your poor potted geranium, making of all hallways
horizons, you animate the inanimate and humanize the human.

II

Only higher than laughter is love, and love I can send you—here
from the northwoods where the frogs by the pond's edge speak
their ancient language,

And the pines stand encircling a savage amphitheatre whose audience
is made up of ghosts and whose players are the marionettes of
moonlight,

Where far down in the valley a slow freight rumbles by, its whistle
a panache guiding in cluttered cars its legions of loneliness
deep into the dark interior.

Thinking of you, I summon completeness and cancel confusion; the
thought of you laughing brings laughter and laughter brings
light;

And clasping and unclasping my hands—your contagious gesture—
in this somber house, I hold a whole spectrum of light

Which breaks within my fingers as on the points of a star,

Each break, a contagion of color, each—through the room, the
house, the mountain and valley—reflecting you, in every
happy aspect, as you were, and are.

A TUNE FOR THE TELETYPE

O Teletype, tell us of time clocks and trouble,
Wheels within wheels, rings within rings;
In each little ring a pretty wire basket,
In each pretty basket any number of things—

Things to be stamped and despatched in good order:
O tell us of code clerks and typists who toil
So the world may receive the good news in the morning,
And H-bombs explode according to Hoyle!

H-bombs explode and each pretty wire basket
With bits of charred paper fly off through the air!
The question is answered, but who's there to ask it?
The man with the question is no longer there.

The question-man now is somewhere in orbit;
He's calling—click-click—the whole human race.
A man in the moon, but no cow to jump over—
End of the poem . . . Space . . . Space . . . Space . . . Space . . .

RANDOM GENERATION OF ENGLISH SENTENCES
OR, THE REVENGE OF THE POETS

Dr. Louis T. Milic of the Columbia University department of English expressed a note of caution about computers. He said that attention might be diverted to secondary work and that the nature of literature might be distorted if computers changed matters that were essentially qualitative into a quantitative form.

But Professor Milic admitted that computers are improving—perhaps even to the point of writing poetry as good as that composed by a drunken poet. He cited a sentence generated by a group from the Massachusetts Institute of Technology working with a computer, and contained in a study called, "Random Generation of English Sentences."

The sentence is: "What does she put four whistles beside heated rugs for?"

—*The New York Times*, September 10, 1964

What does she put four whistles beside heated rugs for?
The answer is perfectly clear:
Four drunken poets might reel through the woodwork
And leer.

Four drunken poets might lurch toward the heated rugs,
Bearing buckets of ice,
And say: "Madam, it's colder than your computer may think;
Our advice

Is to pick up your whistles and fold your tents like the Arabs
And silently steal—or fly—
Where all your hot-rugged brothers and sisters are headed.
Madam, good-bye!"

PIDGIN PINCH

Joe, you Big Shot! You Big Man!
You Government Issue! You Marshall Plan!

Joe, you got plenty Spearmint Gum?
I change you Money, you gimme Some!

Joe, you want Shoe-Shine, Cheap Souvenir?
My Sister overhaul you Landing Gear?

Joe, you Queer Kid? Fix-you Me?
Dig-Dig? Buzz-Buzz? Reefer? Tea?

Joe, I find you Belly Dance,
Trip Around the World—Fifty Cents!

Joe, you got Cigarette? Joe, you got Match?
Joe, you got Candy? You Sum-Bitch,

You think I Crazy? I waste my Time?
I give you *Trouble*? Gimme a *Dime*!

THE ANTIMACASSAR
AND THE OTTOMAN

"I am leaving this house as soon as I can,"
Said the Antimacassar to the Ottoman.
"I hate this room, I loathe this chair,
I can't stand people's oily hair,
I long for a breath of mountain air.
      I will fly away to Turkistan;
      Will you come with me, dear Ottoman?"

The Ottoman sighed and said: "Oh, man!
I will certainly go with you if I can.
I, too, am sick of this overstuffed chair
And want nothing more than a breath of air!
I'm weary of having my praises sung
By an ugly pot of Mother-in-law's tongue!
Give me a mountain's twisted shapes
For the arsenic green of those green drapes;
Give me the green of a foreign land
For the green of that green umbrella stand!
I daily see a dreadful menace
In that awful painted scene of Venice
That glows at night like dead desire
Above an artificial fire.
I know by heart the sad tweet-tweets
Of those pale sky-blue parakeets!
And all I can hear is a high-pitched snicker
From that chaise longue of painted wicker!
The African violets are wet,
They haven't dried their pink eyes yet;
Day after day their hot tears come
Across the cold linoleum!
They *loathe* this room as much as I!
      Tears, idle tears! *I* cannot cry.
      Do let us go—do let us fly!"

But an Ottoman it cannot fly,
And an Antimacassar—who knows why?—
Is pinned in permanence to a chair.
So when morning came, they both were there;
And no window opened to let in the air,
     And neither had flown to Turkistan—
     The Antimacassar nor the Ottoman.

BAY-BREASTED BARGE BIRD

The bay-breasted barge bird delights in depressions
And simply flourishes during slumps;
It winters on hummocks near used-car lots
      And summers near municipal dumps.

It nests on the coils of old bed springs,
And lines its nest with the labels from cans;
It feeds its young on rusty red things,
      And bits of pots and pans.

The bay-breasted barge bird joyfully passes
Where bulldozers doze and wreckers rumble,
Gazing bug-eyed, when traffic masses,
      At buildings that feather and crumble.

It wheels and dips to the glare and thunder
Of blasted rock and burning fuel
While the red-hot riveted sun goes under
      On every urban renewal.

It flaps long wings the color of soot,
It cranes a neck dotted with purple bumps;
And lets out a screech like a car in a crack-up
      As it slowly circles the dumps.

BALLAD OF THE
LADY QUID PRO QUO

I

On the Coasts of Consternation,
   Through a mournful field of snow,
     On a piebald circus steed,
   Rode the Lady Quid Pro Quo.
Dressed in domino demurely,
Reins held loosely but securely,—
     Through a melancholy mead,
     On a piebald circus steed,
     At a chaste and modest speed
   Rode the Lady Quid Pro Quo,
   Rode the Lady Quid Pro Quo.

II

"Lady Quid!" I called out clearly,
   And I heard my voice echo,
     "Tell me, will you, why so rides
   Lovely Lady Quid Pro Quo;
Why sedately and discreetly,
Unconcerned with life completely,
     Why, above its changing tides,
     So symbolically rides,
     Desolation on all sides,
   Lovely Lady Quid Pro Quo,
   Lovely Lady Quid Pro Quo?"

III

She reined in, saying: "You have asked me
   Why I keep to this limbo?
     There may be things worth living for,"
   Said the Lady Quid Pro Quo:
"Sweetness, light, hush puppies, honey,
Duck soup, cream puffs, mushrooms, money,—

There may be things worth living for,
But there are many, many more
Whose existence I deplore!"
Said the Lady Quid Pro Quo,
Said the Lady Quid Pro Quo.

IV

I stood dumbfounded; she continued
(Her steed distracted pawed the snow):
"O there are horrors I'd have banned!"
Said the Lady Quid Pro Quo.
"Ad *infinitum* suburbs sprawling,
Bombs exploding, fallout falling,
Spoken German, music canned,
British cooking, bleary, bland,—
Wholesale horrors I'd have banned!"
Said the Lady Quid Pro Quo,
Said the Lady Quid Pro Quo.

V

"Horrors daily omnipresent
Met at midnight or cockcrow—
Airplanes writing in midair,"
Said the Lady Quid Pro Quo,
"Hipsters, hucksters babbling brightly,
TV bushwa beamed out nightly,—
Mannequins in underwear,
Airplanes writing in midair,
Unfurling brands of underwear!"
Said the Lady Quid Pro Quo,
Said the Lady Quid Pro Quo.

VI

"Things enough!"—she cried intensely,
And clutched her fraying domino.—
"Sick jokes, gadgets, and baseball,"
Cried the Lady Quid Pro Quo.
"Things that roil me, rack me, gnaw me,

Corny, crummy, and gewgawy,—
    I could do without them all,
        Sick jokes, gadgets, and baseball,
        And other items large and small!"
    Cried the Lady Quid Pro Quo,
    Cried the Lady Quid Pro Quo.

VII

"Things—I'd list them if I wanted"—
    And her list began to grow—
        "Statisticians, actuaries,"
    Said the Lady Quid Pro Quo,
"Fallout falling, killers killing,
Dozers dozing, dentists drilling,
        Statisticians, actuaries,
        Birch-inflamed reactionaries,
        Plastic bags, and dead canaries!"
    Said the Lady Quid Pro Quo,
    Said the Lady Quid Pro Quo.

VIII

"Lady Quid Pro Quo," I countered,
    "You are justified, although
        If such things abound," I said
    To the Lady Quid Pro Quo,
"Then there can be no reshaping,
Compromising nor escaping.
        If such things abound," I said.
        "You were really *better* dead,
        However justified," I said
    To the Lady Quid Pro Quo,
    To the Lady Quid Pro Quo.

IX

Without concern or consternation,
    Her voice an eerie undertow,
        Her eyes careening like her steed,
    Cried the Lady Quid Pro Quo:
"I agree on that point gladly!"

(Here she twirled her horsewhip madly)
  And wild-eyed grew her piebald steed.
  "I were *better* dead indeed,
  On *that* point we are agreed!"
 Cried the Lady Quid Pro Quo,
 Cried the Lady Quid Pro Quo.

X

Then off to what dim destination,
 Off, swirling in her checked poncho,
  Goaded by what hidden goad,
 Rode the Lady Quid Pro Quo.
Off, sedately and discreetly,
Unconcerned with life completely,
  Off into the blizzard rode,
  Goaded by what hidden goad,
  Off laconically rode
 Lovely Lady Quid Pro Quo,
 Lovely Lady Quid Pro Quo.

XI

On the Coasts of Consternation,
 Swathed in sheets like drifting snow,
  I awoke then on this bed,
 Examining the status quo.
Nerve ends frayed, blood pressure rising,
Life, dear life, almost despising,
  I awoke and held my head
  Here on this crazy-quilted bed,
  Not a thought inside my head
 Save of that Lady Quid Pro Quo,
 Save of that Lady Quid Pro Quo.

V

The Tin Can

THE TIN CAN

One very good thing I have learned from writer friends in Japan is that when you have a lot of work to do, especially writing, the best thing is to take yourself off and hide away. The Japanese have a word for this, the "kanzume," or the "tin can," which means about what we would mean by the "lock-up." When someone gets off by himself to concentrate, they say, "He has gone into the tin can."

      —HERBERT PASSIN, "The Mountain Hermitage: Pages from a Japanese Notebook," *Encounter*, August 1957.

I

I have gone into the tin can; not in late spring, fleeing a stewing,
      meat-and-fish smelling city of paper houses,

Not when wisteria hangs, a purple cloud, robbing the pines of
      their color, have I sought out the gray plain, the indeterminate
      outer edge of a determined world,

Not to an inn nestling astride a waterfall where two mountains
      meet and the misty indecisiveness of Japanese ink-drawn pines
      frames the afternoon, providing from a sheer bluff an adequate
      view of infinity,

But here to the tin can in midwinter: to a sagging New England
      farmhouse in the rock-rooted mountains, where wind rifles the
      cracks,

Here surrounded by crosshatched, tumbling stone walls, where
      the snow plow with its broad orange side-thrust has outlined
      a rutted road,

Where the dimly cracked gray bowl of the sky rests firmly on the
      valley and gum-thick clouds pour out at the edges,

Where in the hooded afternoon a pock-marked, porcupine-
      quilled landscape fills with snow-swirls, and the tin can settles
      in the snow.

I have gone into the tin can, head high, resolute, ready to confront
      the horrible, black underside of the world.

Snow-murmur! Wind-dip! Heart-rage! It is now my duty to
    record, to enumerate, to set down the sounds, smells, meanings
    of this place . . .

How begin? With the red eye of the chocolate-brown rhinoceros?
    With the triple-serrated teeth of the pencil-fed monster with
    bright fluted ears and whirling black tail? . . .

There is a skittering and scrambling in the can: a trickle of sand
    and sawdust from a sack, wet leaves blown back, cracks spreading
    along the wall.

There is the chitter and clatter of keys, a smudge of pencils, a
    smear of time . . .

Stippled heaven! Snow-ruffle! Garnet-groove! Black water winding
    through snow-wounds! Ripple-roost!

Will the wilds wake? Will the words work? Will the rattle and
    rustle subside? Will the words rise?

A bluejay flashes by a window, the stripes of his tail, chevrons
    torn from a noncom's sleeve; and in the afternoon the snow
    begins.

First: a hush—pit-stillness, black accent of hemlocks up and down
    the mountain, mist in the valley thickening and deepening
    until it breaks

And the snow already fallen swirls up to meet the snow descending—
    sky-darkening, still-deepening, sky-hooded and whirling,
    flakes flying,

Houses settling sidewise in the drifts—winds wedging, snow-
    choked road lost, still-winding, earth white-star-carpeted, still-
    wheeling;

And in the tin can the same still, paper-white, damp emptiness.

                            II

A door opens—is it a door?—and a woman walks by in the tin
    can watering tropical plants that jut from the wall or spring
    from the floor, their leaves great green famished mouths,—

Feeding the fish, distributing specks to the seahorses in their tank
and meat to the turtle on his wet pillow;

Cats curling about her legs, she pats the dogs and caresses the
heads of the children, and the children open their green mouths
and grow upward toward the sunlight like plants.

A door opens: a woman walks by, and through her bobbing,
mud-colored glass watches the movements of my pencil,

And a record turns, a black hemstiched whirlpool, and the
woman wheels off in a trance of drumbeats, screaming of need
and nothingness and money;

And money like wet leaves piles high around my ankles, and I am
sickened by its smell . . .

Snow-madness! Leaf-mania! Green parabolas! In the tin can
there is no morning of revelation, no afternoon of appraisal, no
evening of enchantment.

In the tin can a small boy in a nightmare kicks one leg from the
bed overturning a glowing iron stove, and in seconds fire
sweeps through a city of tin cans.

I wake thinking of the boy, and all about me are the smoking
ruins of cigarettes; and the ashes descend through the half-
extinguished afternoon with the smell of burning flesh . . .

A weasel waddles along in a kind of trotting walk; a mole inches
up through darkness, his blind trail, the workings of consciousness.

In the tin can I hear a murmur of voices speaking of the life in other
tin cans, of death sifting through them.

A vision of bodies blasted on the black earth; and I think of those
photographs my father kept from the Nicaraguan Insurrection,
was it?—that we played with as children on a sun-spotted
floor—

Brown bodies spread out over the jungle floor, the figures beside
them wide-eyed and bewildered, toy soldiers in ridiculous
stances in a meaningless world;

I think of the photographs rubbed vinegar-brown in the sunlight;
  and of how we placed them around us, lined our toy fortress
  with them,

And talked to one another through tin-can telephones, while
  from out the photographs the jungle's green arm tapped our
  small brown shoulders.

III

The tin can is circling with beasts: dogs howl in the night, cats
  sidle through slats in the tin, wet field mice hanging from their
  mouths;

I step in the morning over the entrails of rodents lying like spun
  jewels on the carpet, offerings to the dark gods.

And the dogs rise from their corners, their dirt-crusted rag beds,
  smelling of snow, sniffing the roots, digging the floor, and
  begin again to circle the can . . .

Bright flashes of morning! Blue snow-peaks! Fog smoking the
  valleys! Angels lighting the rubble! Children skating on a blue
  pond! Deer stepping delicately down through the pines! . . .

And always the face, the woman's face, brooding over all, rising
  from the earth beside me, disembodied; always the woman
  clean and classic as sunlight, moving about the room, sifting
  the dirt, watering the shadowy flowers, polishing the spotted
  tin.

I hear her speak softly; and there she is again beside me; and again
  the face turns, a small bat-face and the lips draw back in a red
  wound and shriek; and the room is filled with a smell of mould
  and money . . .

The woman turns, the bat-face again a woman's face blue with
  shrieking, and the woman walks to the end of the corridor,
  climbs a broad white stairway . . .

Leaf-fringe! Sky-tingle! Cloud-clatter! Earth-blaze! All my under-
  world crumbles; and I am left with the one brooding face,
  no face; with bat-wings folding the black air into a shroud.

IV

When am I to emerge? Dirt falls; eyes blur; memory confounds;
multiple voices move furred and batlike round my ears; and
then no sound—

Only the grating of a pencil over a page—an army of ant words
swarming up to consciousness.

When will they break through to a bright remembered world, up
through the top of the tin?

Snow-swirl—hemlocks hunching toward the window—gray-
black shadow cutting over black, fan shaken over fan . . .

From here the windows open their white mouths to swallow the
wind-driven snow.

And I remember salmon sky, fine-boned sunsets sweeping the
spiny mountains; and I have seen the snow

In banks driven back from the road, the black edges scraggly and
bearded, the snowbanks under the birches like milk from
buckets overturned and frozen . . .

Will the words rise? Will the poem radiate with morning? Here
where I see nothing, I have seen the Cyclops-eye ballooning
over a frozen world,

The wide fringe of eyelashes opening on all existence, the single
glazed dazzle of the eye watching,

And I have lived with my eyes—watching the watching eye, the
eyeball swivelling in nothingness, a huge black moon in egg-
white immensity.

And I have seen the edges of the tin can fold in around it.

V

O bodies my body has known! Bodies my body has touched and
remembered—in beds, in baths, in streams, on fields and streets
—will you remember?

Sweet vision of flesh known and loved, lusted after, cherished,
repulsed, forgotten and remembered, will you remember my
body buried now and forgotten? . . .

In childhood we played for hours in the sun on a dump near a
        cannery; and the long thin ribbons of tin rippled round us,
        and we ran by the railroad track and into the backyard behind
        the asparagus and through the feathers of green our bodies
        touched and the strips of tin radiated their rainbows of light—

And our bodies were spiralled with tin and wondrous with light—

Now out of darkness here from the tin can, through snow-swirl
        and wind-dazzle, let the tin ribbons ride again and range in
        new-found freedom;

Let the tin rip and rustle in the wind; let the green leaves rise and
        rift the wondrous windows, leaving behind the raging women,
        and the sickening mould of money, rust, and rubble . . .

And the words clean-spun and spiralling orbit that swift-seeing,
        unseen immensity that will never be contained!